SOCIOLOGY

LOVE SUSTAINS ALL: THE SOCIOLOGY OF LOVE

BY

M.F. ONUCHUKWU

© 2019

To My Creator,

I give all majesty for blessing

me with the wisdom to express

a figment of his unending love

in black and white.

Preface

The reader must endeavor to study this book with the mind that he has never read a subject matter on love.

The reader must also try to relate the contents of this book with his real experiences in life to better aid his understanding of the book material.

The reader must definitely do well to have a first hand understanding of the definition of sociology.

Table of Contents

Love Isn't Selfish – Chapter 1

A person who loves someone cares about him or her. When you love someone you're always concerned about their needs, welfare and living conditions. To love is to be selfless. One who loves is always glad to see that others are in a better condition than him. To love is to believe that others deserve better than you. It is to give when it's convenient for you. It's to show sincere concern for the plight of others. It's to live in the service of others. A person who loves someone is always joyful to see that the needs of the person that he loves are catered for. His body becomes stronger whenever he sees that the desires of the ones he loves are being catered for. The mind of someone who loves another becomes very active and his thoughts very clearer whenever he sees that the needs of the person he cares for are being provided. When you love someone you channel your thoughts more towards their well being than yours. The nature of love makes it impossible to love without selflessness.

When a man loves a woman all he cares about is satisfying all her needs. The same goes for the woman. A man who truly loves a woman caters for her bodily, mental and spiritual needs. A man who loves a woman ensures that he provides for her basic bodily needs like her sexual and financial needs. He ensures that he provides for her basic

mental needs through encouraging

positive daily discourses. Such a man

directs his mental energies towards

edifying the mind of the woman he loves

by encouraging her to study and

understand books which stimulate

positive and active thoughts. A man

shows care towards the woman he loves

by guiding her towards a lasting

relationship with her Creator. He always

displays true concern for her spirituality.

A man who truly loves a woman will put

her needs first before his. He loves her and as a result isn't selfish towards her. Whenever a man sees the woman he loves, he experiences profound joy. His body becomes stronger and his thoughts become very clear and active.

In a family where love exists, there's a mutual feeling of selflessness among the members of the family. Everyone in the family cares about the plight of each other sincerely. In such a family where love exists, everyone looks out for themselves. They all seek to satisfy the needs of one another first before their individual needs. The father always seeks to satisfy the bodily, mental and spiritual needs of the mother and the children before his. The mother in turn seeks to satisfy his bodily, mental and spiritual needs and those of the children first before hers. In a family where there's true love, the children always want to satisfy the bodily, mental and spiritual needs of their parents. They deeply care about their parents and won't stop until they see that the welfare and life conditions of their parents are catered for before theirs. The physical bodies of such family members become stronger as a result of their selfless actions towards one another. Their thoughts also become very clear and active as a result of the love they display towards one another.

The community is another arena of life where love ought to exist. When love is in the community, all the families that make up the communities see to the provision of the basic needs of the families that don't have such needs before theirs. The people making up such communities form social groups that see to the provision of the needs of those who don't have. The families making up such communities selflessly take up projects like the building of court houses, markets, town halls, water storage tanks, libraries and churches. Through these projects they cater for the bodily, mental and spiritual needs of the members of the communities. The members of such a community are always joyous whenever they see each other. They understand that love has made them put aside their own appetites so that the appetites of others may be satisfied. When the members of such a community see each other, their bodies become stronger and their minds very active because of the selflessness towards one another.

The organization that has its principal foundation as love shall always have its members looking out for the needs of each other. Such an organization will have people who always put others before themselves in all spheres of life. The members of an organization who love each other always seek to meet the bodily, mental and spiritual needs of each other. They seek to build an ergonomically viable environment for those who work in the organization. The management of the organization pay the workers on time. The workers are guided to the pinnacle of their profession through understanding based training. Psycho-spiritual counselors are made available to them to aid their spiritual needs at the workplace.

Through the various selfless measures put in place at the workplace, the members of the organization become stronger in the body. They're very joyful when they help each other to meet their various needs in the organization. Their minds become very clear and their thoughts active due to their selflessness.

A nation rooted in love always has a citizenry that's conscious of being selfless. The citizens of such a nation look for active ways to help each other satisfy their various needs. They care for themselves and in the process cements the love that flows at the individual, familial, communal and organizational levels. A nation built on love has a citizenry that promotes equality. Such a nation has a citizenry that unites through love to fight the horrors of division and corruption. A nation that has citizens who love each other adopts a national constitution founded on liberty, justice and truth. When love permeates a nation, the citizenry puts the good of their nation before their own good. When love guides a nation, they engage in developmental driven projects like creating jobs, improving their military, providing quality healthcare for their citizens as well as fighting illiteracy.

The citizens of a nations where love flows freely rejoice whenever they help their fellow citizens. Their bodies become stronger and their minds more active because of the love that they express.

At the international level, when love flows globally, nations relate with one another from the ideological perspective of selflessness. Nations grant aids to other countries in need. They work together to achieve the common goal of promoting global peace through understanding. When nations love each other, they ensure that they satisfy the needs of other nations bodily, mentally and spiritually. Nations in love unite to ensure that other nations in need are aided financially through prompt international grants and aids that will alleviate the sufferings of the people of such nations. The love that flows between nations ensures that they take stringent measures to avoid wars and catastrophes on a global scale only through understanding. When nations unite in love, they look out for the common enemy called selfishness. A world (an earth) built on love shall last eternally. Nations that unite in love always seek for ways to improve the world. They unite in love to fight tyranny, colonialism, imperialism and global injustices. In love, global courts with branches in all the nations of the world are established to check the excesses of and hold accountable world leaders who rule their people in selfishness. A world where love flows freely shall know nothing like suffering. It shall be a world where joy and happiness is displayed when the peoples of the different nations help each other selflessly. The bodies of the people inhabiting the earth becomes stronger and their minds clearer and active.

Love Doesn't Delight In Evil – Chapter 2

If you love someone, you wouldn't want to rejoice when you see them get hurt bodily, mentally and/or spiritually. The love a person has for another will never allow him think of anything unpleasant happening to the person that he loves. When you love someone, you'll always feel pain in a magnified capacity when something evil and terrible ensure causes them bodily harm. You'll feel much sorrows when they're exposed mentally to evil discourse or learning materials that will damage their mental health. A person who loves someone will always become distraught as well as feel pain when he discovers that the one he loves is being attacked spiritually. The nature of love ensures that no matter the situation one can never see to the harm of who he loves. Love has nothing to do with evil and anyone who loves

another person can never rejoice when

the person gets hurt or something

unpleasant happens to the person. When

you love someone and something evil

happens to the person whom you love,

you feel unhappy and distraught. You

feel very sorrowful when something

unpleasant occurs to someone whom

you love. Your body becomes very weak

when you see something bad happen to

someone you love. You can't reason or

think clearly and your thoughts become

very passive when you come to the knowledge that something bad has happened to the one you love.

How can a man claim to love a woman if he doesn't care about if the woman is hurt or has come to harm? A man truly loves a woman if he feels pain whenever he sees the woman in distress. He doesn't rest his body a bit until he sees that the woman gets out of the pain and becomes okay. The same goes for a woman's love for a man. A man recognizes that he owes it to the woman to ensure that he feels pained when something evil happens to her. It's out of love for a woman that a man feels pained when she comes to hurt. A man becomes very sorrowful when he sees that the woman he loves has come to hurt in the body or mind or spirit. Bodily speaking, a man is pained when he perceives that the woman he loves has been met with a bodily accident. A man becomes distraught when he discovers that the woman he loves has also come to experience mental trauma and/or in the process has become very mentally unstable. He doesn't take a break until he sees to it that the woman he loves has become okay and has returned to normalcy. Also a man who loves a woman becomes very sad when he sees her suffering spiritually from malign spirits. However, because of the love he has for her, he ensures that she gets spiritual help urgently. A man's body becomes very weak when he perceives that harm has come to the woman he loves. He can't think clearly or have active thoughts anymore when he receives news that something evil has happened to the one he loves.

The family is the place where deep love ought to be displayed among family members. A father doesn't eat or drink for days or even months when he discovers that bodily harm has come to his wife and children. A father loves his wife and children and will never take joy to the fact that they've hurt their physical bodies. In the same vein, when something unpleasant happens to her husband or children, a mother becomes very sorrowful and displays her sorrows by losing bodily appetite. A father comes to serious grief when he discovers that the his family has been exposed to hideous discourse and/or learning materials that have the capacity of damaging their mental health. The same goes for the mother who will never delight in the evil that happens to her family. Also, a father's love for his family will never allow him delight in their sufferings caused by malign spirits. A father becomes very sorrowful whenever he sees his family come under attack spiritually. The same goes for the mother of the family. The children are not left out in the scheme of love. The children are saddened when their parents come to harm bodily or mentally or spiritually. They feel much pain on hearing that something unpleasant has happened to their parents. When the members of a family love each other, their bodies become very weak when anyone among them comes to harm. Their minds become hazed with passiveness and grief; and they don't think clearly.

Each family that makes up a community where love flows freely feel sorrowful when they come to the knowledge that evil has befallen a particular family. They don't rejoice when they hear that a family in the community is experiencing pain. Rather, they grieve with such a family and become sorrowful as a result of the harm which has come to them. In such a community where love exists, there are house visitations to those who have come to harm by members of the community and words of encouragement are shared with them; gifts are also sent to them with letters of concern and healing; funds are raised by the members of the community to alleviate such families of their sufferings. In a community where love flows, there's much joy and happiness. When people help others end the evil that's plaguing them their bodies become stronger and their minds become very clear and active.

When an organization has love as its guiding principles, the members of such an organization always look out for each other. They feel very distraught when they discover that any member of the organization has been met with harm. As a result of the love which permeates the very fabric of the organization, emergency response systems are made available in the event of a worker getting bodily hurt. There's also hospital visitation days to a worker who has come to bodily harm. The organization sees to it that any worker who gets hurt while on duty gets his full pay despite being absent from the job. Support and encouragement is shown to workers who've mentally suffered work traumas by co-workers and the organization. Psycho-spiritual counselors employed by the organization feel very saddened when they learn that a worker is under attack spiritually. They do everything in their power to help them from their spiritual calamities. The members of an organization where love has taken preeminence feel very sad when they come to know that one of them has had something very unpleasant happen to them. Their bodies become very weak and their minds become dulled and passive when they receive such news.

The nation is a place where love ought to be epitomized. The citizens of a nation where love exists always feel much sorrows when they learn that other citizens of the nation has come to harm. The same goes for the government of a nation where love is the order of the day. In a nation where love exists citizens always feel very sad when they see that their fellow citizen(s) has come to harm bodily or mentally or spiritually. When a citizen has come to harm body wise, the citizens of such a nation mourn and take it upon themselves to see that he who

has come to harm receives relief. Also,

if the citizens of a nation where love

flows freely like water running down a

cliff discover that their fellow citizens is

suffering from severe mental trauma,

they feel very distraught and do

everything in their might to ensure that

such a citizen receives the care needed

for him to recuperate back to good

mental health. Likewise when the

citizens of a nation discover that there

are other citizens in the nation that are

suffering spiritually, they don't rejoice but get sad at such discovery. They offer such a citizen help as much as they can and ensure that they become alright at the end of the day. In such a nation, the government provides proper national emergency centers that respond to sufferings of those who've been hurt. They provide financial assistance and relief for the family of those who've been hurt while serving the nation. The government of such a nation where love is being out poured freely on a daily provide National Mental Health Trauma centers where those who suffer mentally are being taken care of. The government of such a nation formulates policies that promote religion-spiritual liberties that ensure that institutions are built that cater for the psycho-spiritual well being of their citizens. The citizens of such a nation feel much sorrows and pains when they come to the knowledge that something very unpleasant has happened to their fellow citizens. Their bodies become very weak and their thoughts become very passive when they receive

the news that something evil happened

to their fellow citizen.

Internationally, when nations love each

other, they look out for themselves.

When love reigns supreme in the world,

nations feel very sad when they see

other nations in distress. Nations don't

find joy in the fact that evil has befallen

another nation in a world full of love. In

a world where love is paramount,

nations look out for other nations bodily,

mentally and spiritually. An earth where

the nations of the world feel very sad when the peoples of other nations of the world come to harm either bodily or mentally or spiritually is one full of love. In a world filled with love, nations feel distraught when they see the peoples occupying other nations of the world suffer from famine, pestilence, financial hardships and bodily diseases. They provide assistance to the agricultural bodies in these nations, foreign grants and loans as well as international health emergency centers.

The nations experience much sorrows when they see other nations of the world being subjected to mental shocks that come from warfare psychological operations and fake news media. They feel much sadness when they see other nations fall apart mentally. They establish international mental health facilities in these nations to aid those who suffer mental traumas. When love has become the order of the day in the world, nations feel much grief when they see other nations suffer spiritually.

They provide these other nations of the world with psycho-spiritual counselors who would in turn train other psycho-spiritual counselors in those nations of the world. The peoples of nations of the world feel very dejected when they see the peoples of other nations of the world suffer as a result of evil. The bodies of the peoples of these nations of the world become very weak and their minds dulled as well as their thoughts become passive and unclear; when they discover that their something unpleasant has happened to other nations of the world.

Love Always Trusts – Chapter 3

If you love someone, you always believe that he is good. You believe that he is honest and sincere. You believe that they're straight in their dealings. When you love someone you believe in the good in them. You always trust the one you love no matter what. When you love someone you accept what they say because you believe that they're expressing themselves as they really feel. When someone loves another, he doesn't consider that the person he loves can be dishonest or insincere. When you love someone you believe and take as truth what they tell you. You don't remotely consider that they can lie to you. When love exists between two people they trust themselves bodily or mentally or spiritually. They always believe that both their bodily language are sincere. They believe that their thoughts are honest. Their spirits agree on all things because they believe in each other. If you see someone you trust, your body becomes stronger and your thoughts get into active mode.

The love which exists between a man and woman is meant to be one based on trust. A man loves a woman because he believes that she's a good person. He believes that she's honest in her dealings with him. He believes in the sincerity she displays. He never harbors the thought of her ever being crooked with him. He believes in her and the fact that she can never lie to him. The same goes for a woman who loves a man. The love a man has for a woman makes him have absolute confidence in her body wise, mental wise and spiritual wise. When love guides the relationship between a man and a woman, the man always trusts the body language of the woman. When they communicate with their bodies, they exude the confidence they've in themselves. A man who loves a woman ensures that no matter the situation, their body languages convey honesty and sincerity. When love becomes the pillar of the mutual relations between a man and a woman, their thoughts convey total believe in each other. They don't doubt their abilities to handle the issues that confront them together. They're always trusting their minds. When a man loves a woman, he discovers that he trusts the yearnings of her spirit. He absolutely believes in everything her spirit communicates to him. A man notices that whenever he sees the woman he believes in, his body becomes stronger and his mind very alert. He comes to a realization that his thoughts have suddenly become very active.

Is it possible to imagine the kind of trust that exists in a family where love flows freely? 'It's impossible to do so', I tell you especially if you consider the fact that each member of the family completely believe that others are good.

A father believes that the mother and children in the family are honest. He believes that they act sincerely with him when they deal with them. He isn't suspicious of them in anyway and believes absolutely what they say as truth. In a family where love exists, the mother acts in the same manner to the father and her children. She absolutely believes whatever he says and never for once asks questions about the straightforwardness of his statements.

Where such love exists, the children regard the statements of their parents as truth. They see their parents as good people that are completely honest and sincere. The members of the family where love exists completely trust themselves bodily, mentally and spiritually. Such a family has members that respond to each other through a body communication that portrays confidence in themselves. They believe in themselves, thus they give and seek financial assistance from one another. A family where love exists always trust in their mental abilities to solve the problems that they face daily. Such a family believes that each person in the family has the capacity to solve the problems that beguile them. A family where love exists becomes a family where they trust each other to edify their spirits through divine words of guidance which they speak to one another. It's a family where they trust each other to meet their various spiritual needs. It's a family where the belief in the potentials of one another to be faithful remains the

enduring ethos. When the members of

such a family meet up, their bodies

become stronger and their minds

sharpened as a result of their mutual

trust among themselves. The conceive

only active thoughts when they're

together.

A community where love is the

forerunner of the inter-relations between

the families that make up the community

becomes one where the members of the

community trust one another to remain good and faithful as they relate. It's one where the members of the community absolutely believe in each other. It's one where the members of the community relate to one another with all sincerity of purpose. In such a community, families are always honest in their dealings with one another. The members of such a community where love reigns supreme ensures that they relate with one another in mutual trust; either body or mental or spiritual wise. Such members of a community trust each other to actively respond to threats which they may face. The families making up the community where love flows freely trust each other to actively help in building a mentally sound community where proper education remains an everlasting priority. A community where love reigns is one where the members of the community believe in one another to build spiritual institutions that will help other members of the community when they've spiritual needs. Found in these communities are members who on a constant basis show that they believe that other members are good, faithful and very reliable when dealing with them. When members of the community deal with other members of the community in trust, their bodies become stronger and their minds very active.

Organizations that follow the path of love always create an environment of trust where members of the organization learn to believe in the good in other members of the organization. There's no time to be cynical in such a work environment where members have learnt to trust in the abilities of others bodily, mentally and spiritually. In such organizations workers communicate effectively through sincere body language that helps productivity in the workplace. Such an organization provides proper workplace training assistance where members who properly understand the job trust train and coach other members and trusting them to become efficient and proficient on the job like them. In the same vein, workers trust the organization to provide proper psycho-spiritual counseling for them when they're down and out spiritually.

The workers in such an organization rejoice when they relate with each other because of the mutual trust they've in one another. When they come across themselves at any point in time, their bodies become stronger and their minds alert. Their thoughts become very active because they believe in each other.

A nation where love reigns is one where the citizens become very reliable in their outlook. It's one where the citizens can depend on each other because they trust each other. It's one where the citizens are honest in their relations with one another. It's one where the government through sincerity of purpose delivers good governance to the people. It's one where the people of the nation believes in the ability of government to be accountable, transparent and corruption free. Such a nation is one where the people follow the rule of law because they trust in their constitution. A nation where love is dominant is one where the citizens and the government hold each other responsible to believe in the good which they can all offer. When love becomes the order of the day in a nation, citizens trust their capabilities bodily, mentally and spiritually. They don't doubt for once that they are capable of solving their problems. In a nation where love reigns supreme, citizens trust their capabilities to aid others in their quest to keep themselves very safe and healthy. Such a nation harbor citizens that think logically. They ensure that the government provides facilities that care for those who're mentally traumatized. The citizens of such a nation ensure that they provide psycho-spiritual help for those citizens that are plagued by the influence of malign spirit. They encourage the government to create institutions that cater for the spiritual needs of other citizens. When the citizens of a nation where love makes them live in trust see one another, they become very joyous. Whenever, they see themselves, their bodies become stronger and their thoughts become very active.

A world where the nations interact out of love is one where the nations believe that they're good and honest. It's one where the nations deal with each other in a straightforward manner. It's one where the nations live in the understanding that other nations are inherently good. Such a nation, where love exists becomes very aware of the fact that crookedness is to be avoided in the relations between nations. The love which exists between such nations make them have a strong believe in the goodness, honesty and sincerity which they exude body wise, mental wise and spiritual wise. In a world where love is the mainstay, nations always provide food assistance to other nations of the world where there's famine and pestilence. The nations of the world protect the human

rights of the citizens of other nations in a

global atmosphere of love especially that

of women. In a world where love rules,

the nations of the world team up to fight

global poverty and birth mortality rates

in other nations of the world where

they're absent. When love takes the lead

on earth, the nations of the world build

mental health facilities in other nations

of the world where mental traumas are

high. They pool resources together to

build schools where logical reasoning is

learned as an art. The nations of the world in love build spiritual institutions where men are taught the art of spiritual healing and acquiring eternal life. When the peoples of the nations of the world come across those nations of the world whom they trust, they become very happy. Their bodies become very strong and the thoughts they think very complete and active.

Love Always

Hopes – Chapter 4

To love is to hope. When you love someone you always feel joy whenever you think about something that happened in their past or future which you're uncertain about. Love always ensures that despite the doubts you've about someone you still feel joy about them whenever you recall them to mind. Hope is the bedrock of love. It's what drives love and makes it certain. A person who loves another always hopes that the person he loves shall become better and if better that he shall become perfect. When love conquers, hope remains the most important theme and is certainly a characteristic of love that defines the conviction that love brings with it. When love hopes, everything becomes certain. Doubts are completely removed even if they appear to be there. When a person loves another, he hopes that he will become better bodily, mentally and spiritually. Where love exists between two persons, they always hope that they'll both earn better incomes and become healthier persons. They hope that they'll both improve their understanding with time and get rid of the thoughts of the past which cause mental traumas. When love leads the way between two persons, they always

hope to reach the pinnacle of their faith

and spirituality. They hope to become

more clairaudient and clairvoyant. If you

love someone you hope will become

better, when you come across them,

your body becomes stronger and your

thoughts become very active.

The love between a man and a woman

makes them hope that they'll both

become better and valuable to each

other. It makes them feel joy when they

ponder about their past and future which

they'd at one time doubted. When a man loves a woman he hopes that she'll become a better woman. He hopes that their relationship will wax stronger. When a man loves a woman, he becomes a partaker of her dreams and aspirations. Where love is the forerunner of all things, a man always feels happiness when he thinks about what their past had offered them together and what what the future holds for them. A man who loves a woman hopes that she'll become better bodily, mentally and spiritually. He hopes that she'll become a fitter and healthier woman. He also hopes that she'll become more sexually active. A man who loves a woman hopes that the woman becomes more logical in her reasoning. He hopes that she filters and screens the type of information that she receives to avoid severe mental health breakdown. When a man loves a woman, he provides emotional support for her when she needs it most. A man who loves a woman hopes that the woman becomes better through psycho-spiritual counseling. He hopes that the woman grows spiritually everyday and obtains eternal life. When a man sees a woman that he loves and hopes to become better, his body becomes stronger and his thoughts very active.

The members of a family where love meanders freely feel great joy when they reminisce on their past and future experiences which they sometimes doubt. In a family where the members love each other, they always hope that those they love will become better persons regardless of how doubtful they're about the past or future. Such a family becomes purely an epitome of optimism. When love reigns in a family, each member of the family becomes a partaker in the hope that their will be improvement in the family. First off, the father always hopes that the mother and the children will see individual improvements. They all hope that each member of the family will become better bodily, mentally and spiritually. In such a family, the father hopes to provide ample food for the members of his family. He hopes to satisfy the sexual appetites of his wife. When love leads the pack in the family, the father hopes that the parental control he puts on the learning material the children consume prevent them from coming to mental harm. He also hopes to protect his wife from any form of mental traumas. In a family where love is apex, the father through his prayers hopes that the mother and the children will be guided and protected divinely. Through encouraging the members of his family to participate in spiritual activities that edify the spirit, he hopes that they grow spiritually. In such a family where love exists, the members of the family hope that all shall be well with everyone of them, and when they meet up they feel great joy. Their bodies become stronger and their minds very sharpened. The thoughts they think become very active when they meet the one they hope will

become better.

Every person that makes up a

community where love is the norm,

hopes that each member of the

community will see great improvement

in their lives. In such a community, the

members always feel uncommon

happiness when the reflect on the events

that took place or that will take place in

the community which they weren't or

aren't sure of their outcomes. When love

engulfs the hearts of the people of the community, the families that make up the community live in the hope that the community shall become better and witness tremendous progress. The members of such a community understand the need for the persons inhabiting the community to witness tremendous progress bodily, mentally and spiritually. The members of such a community hope that each family in the community will witness a tremendous increase in prosperity. They hope that the infant mortality rate in such communities will decrease drastically as well as the maternal mortality rates. The members of such a community encourage healthy living and eating. When love is the main theme of a community, the members of such a community hope that by building libraries where other members of the community go to educate themselves, they'll become better. The members of a community through conducting mental health awareness seminars hope that other citizens shall become better informed on how to manage mental health stress and traumas. In a community where love reigns supreme, the members of such a community hope that by becoming the custodians of the art of spirituality, they will bring spiritual healing to all and sundry in the community. In such a community where love is paramount, the families that make up the community hope that by providing psycho-spiritual counselors to the people of the community, they shall grow spiritually. When the members of a community where they hope to progress as a result of love come across one another, they become very joyous; and as a result of their joy, their thoughts become more active and less passive.

In an organization where love is the mainstay, the members of such an organization work together in the hope that their labors shall yield them great self-improvement. It's in the spirit of self-improvement that the members of an organization become very joyous

when they conceive the ideas of what

had happened to them or will happen to

them as workers in the organization

which they were very uncertain of. It's

in the spirit of hope in love that the

workers in an organization understand

that by working together they shall end

up bettering themselves and making the

organization progress. The members of

such an organization where love

permeates the workspace always seek to

improve their conditions bodily,

mentally and spiritually. The members of such an organization where love takes the lead hope to increase the productivity of the organization where they work and in the process improve the financial remunerations of the other members of the organization. They maintain a high level of ergonomics that makes the workspace very conducive and interesting for other members of the organization. In an organization where love is crown, the members of the organization hope that the mental health awareness training provided at the workplace will help the workers in managing their mental stress and traumas. When love flows like a stream of water in an organization, the members of the organization hope that by providing psycho-spiritual counselors to help other members of the organization that are afflicted by malign spirits, they will help them find spiritual healing and wholeness. When the members of such an organization that hope that other members can become better come across each other they feel never before seen happiness. They feel elated and their minds become very clear and their thoughts very active.

In a nation where love exists, the citizens of the nation hope that other citizens will become better. The people of the nation always hope that there will be an overall improvement in the lives of the citizens of the nation. They hope that the lives of the other citizens of the nation will be one that brings joy when they recollect future or past events about them which they had sometimes doubted. The citizens of such a nation where love reigns maximum hopes that other citizens of the nation will progress bodily, mentally and spiritually. Where the power of love dwells, the citizens of the nations hope that other people residing in the nation become better when they're provided food assistance during famine and pestilence. The citizens of such nation where love abides ensure that other citizens are provided with the needed shelters and other accommodation facilities if they are homeless or face natural disasters. When love takes the lead, the people of such nations hope that other citizens become better by providing them with the mental healthcare facilities to aid them during mental traumas and crisis. In such a nation where love takes precedence, the citizens of the nation hope that by building spiritual institutions all across the nation, they help them heal and blossom spiritually.

The people of such a nation where out of love hope that other members of the nation progress; are joyful when they meet them. Meeting them makes their bodies stronger and their thoughts become very active.

When the world is filled up with love, the nations of the world always hope that other nations of the world will improve and become better. The nations of the world are happy about the outcome of the events which had taken place in the past or which will take place in the future of which they doubt. The nations of the world that are rooted in love hope that other nations of the world see tremendous improvement in all the spheres of nationhood. These nations where love is the pioneering factor, hope that the people of these other nations of the world become better bodily, mentally and spiritually. In a world where love flows naturally, the nations of the world hope that the aid they give to other nations of the world through food assistance programs and agricultural grants helps them reduce hunger in the nations during times of famine and pestilence. When love is the ruling principal in the world, the nations of the world hope that the foreign loans and grants given to the other nations of the world help them build modern infrastructures. When love is the order of the day on earth, the nations of the world hope that the other nations of the world have mentally healthy citizens by providing them with modern mental health institutions that cater for their needs. In such a world where love beams forth radiantly, the nations of the world provide psycho-spiritual training programs for the other nations of the world that will in turn train the citizens of these other nations to provide proper spiritual guidance and healing for those being afflicted spiritually. When the members of these nations of the world where love makes them always hope, see one another, they become excited, their bodies get stronger and their

thoughts become very active.

Love Rejoices With The Truth – Chapter 5

Love exists between two persons if and

only if they rejoice when anyone of

them confesses or talks about what truly

is obtainable in reality. The love one person has for another is displayed when the person delights only in hearing the one whom he loves say the truth. Love between two persons exists when they both learn how to think and say what exists in reality. When love exists between two people, there's an understanding that the truth need to be told always to themselves. When you love someone, you do everything in your power to always tell them the truth. To rejoice in the truth is one of the ways one who loves another behaves. When you love someone you always rejoice when they understand existence in reality, both bodily, mentally and spiritually. In love, a person ensures that he tells another only the truths that govern the spheres of existence. Such a person out of love helps the other become able to reason logically. Also when you love someone you always tell them spiritual truths. Nothing pleases one who loves another like hearing only the truth from the one he loves.

A man loves a woman because she expresses herself truthfully to him. The same goes for a woman who loves a man, the man also pours out his thoughts before her as it is, holding nothing back or twisting the story. When love exists between a man and a woman, they always tell each other the facts. They never lie to one another. When a man loves a woman, he tells her stuff as it really is in reality. He talks to her about only the things that exist concretely and not in the imagination. When love is paramount in a relationship between a man and a woman, they communicate truthfully via their body language. They don't lie to each other about their sexual desires and fantasies. They also don't lie to themselves about their finances. When love paves the way between a man and a woman, they express their emotions as it is to one another. They don't hide their feelings from one another. If love blazes the trail in the relationship between the opposite sexes, they always work towards ensuring that they provide spiritual support and prayers for one another when they are down and out spiritually. They always encourage one another to grow higher spiritually as well as seek eternal life. When a man sees the woman he loves speak the truth, his body becomes stronger and the thoughts that he harbors very active.

In a family where love is dominant, the father always expects the truth from the mother and the children. He always rejoices because they never fail to tell him anything but the truth. The mother in the same manner is joyous whenever the father and the children tell the truth. She doesn't expect less anyways. The children are also elated whenever they hear their parents say only the things which exist in reality. They are happy when their parents are very factual. When love thrives in a family, the members of such a family always tell themselves nothing but the truth. They rejoice when they all tell each other truths body wise, mental wise, and spiritual wise. In a family where love exists, the members of the family never lie about needing financial help to solve food or housing problems. Also in a family where love is key, the members of the family, always bare the truth to one another about their mental health status. They encourage one another to take up logical reasoning as a study as well as improve their understanding. In such a family, the father always tells the mother and children spiritual truths that edify their spirits. When the members of such a family where love flows freely come across one another, they become very happy because of the truth that they constantly tell one another. Their bodies become stronger and their minds very sharpened as a result of the love that makes them truthful to each other.

Any community where love is champion, always has its members very happy because of the truth that they always tell to themselves. In a community where love is key, the members of the community say things as they are without adding or removing details. They are factual to one another and always tell each other the truth despite the circumstance which they face. When a community dwells in love, the members of the community are tuned to the frequency of truth and reality. They always describe things to one another as it exists in reality. The members of such a community always tell each other truths that govern the sphere of existence bodily, mentally and spiritually. In a community where love is peak, the members of the community inform one another truthfully on their welfare and ask for assistance if they are in need of food, clothing and/or shelter. When love exists in a community, the members of the community look out for one another by telling themselves the truth about the importance of building libraries in the community as well as encouraging literacy. In such a community, where love is perpetual, the members of the community rejoice whenever they tell one another spiritual truths that eventually lead to the building of spiritual institutions in the community. In the spirit of truth that comes from love, when members of the community where truth is told see each other, their bodies become very strong and their minds become very alert alongside their very active thoughts.

An organization where love reigns supreme is one where the members of the organization rejoice in being told the truth and in telling the truth. Such an organization where love drives everything is one which upholds the reality of things. It's an organization that says things as they are in existence. The members of such an organization don't compromise on those values that border around truth. When love is the prime mover of an organization, the members of the organization seek to always tell the truth to the other members of the

organization as it relates to them bodily,

mentally and spiritually. The workers in

such an organization always tell the

truth to one another about their financial

situation and they ask for monetary help

from the organization when they are in

dire need of one. In an organization

where love is out poured freely, the

workers who always tell the truth no

matter the situation, are given

promotions and pay increase by the

management. In such an organization

where love is the ruling force, the management of the organization provide integrity based workplace training to the members of the organization to help them relate with one another truthfully. The workers in turn are very honest with the management as well as with each other about their mental health status and inform one another in truth about any work related mental stress or trauma plaguing them. When love becomes the prevailing theme in an organization, the members of the organization become infatuated with seeking spiritual truths and gaining eternal life as a result. When the members of such an organization meet one another they feel joyous as a result of the truth they tell to themselves. Their bodies become very strong and their thoughts very active when they come across themselves.

A nation where love is the mainstay is one in which the citizens of the nation don't lie to one another but only say the truth as it is. It's one in which the citizens of the nation say things exactly the way it's in reality. They narrate events in accordance with the existence of events in reality. They say things as they exist. In a nation where love reigns supreme, the people of the nation live to always understand things as they are and rejoice whenever others understand things in the same vein. When the citizens of a nation love each other, they don't dwell in falsities or come to quick conclusions based on biases. They always live for the truth and are happy when other citizens do the same. The citizens of a nation where love dwells are always compelled to act in such a manner that they display truth bodily, mentally and spiritually. The people of a nation where love takes precedence always pursue justice. They make it an eternal duty to always follow the path of liberty, equality and justice. When love permeates all spheres of life of a nation, the citizens of the nation uphold righteousness and ensures that other citizens do the same. In such a nation where love is the apex, the citizens of the nation ensure that the other citizens truthfully express their concerns especially when it comes to them having access to good food, clothing and accommodation either during severe and acute emergencies or in the case of long term unemployment. When love takes the lead in such a nation, the citizens of the nation, build educational institutions for other citizens of the nation where logical reasoning is taught. They build libraries as well. In a nation where love dominates, the citizens of the nations as a result of truth, build mental healthcare facilities where other peoples residing in the nation that are mentally traumatized can stay and receive treatment. When love is present, the people of a nation propagate spiritual information that helps the spirit of a man who truthfully desires spiritual guidance and healing. When the citizens of a nation where truth is always appreciated meet up with one another, they rejoice in the truth they confess; their bodies become stronger; and their minds clearer as well. Their thoughts come out of passivity and becomes very active.

The nations of the world are always elated when they discover that they relate with one another in truth. In a world where love abounds, the nations of the world live in truth and say things exactly as they exist in reality. They don't say things or act out of their imagination. When love becomes the order of the day in the world, the nations of the world only deal with the facts. They dwell in the realm of certainty. A world where love exists harbors nations that live in truth and which seeks other nations to also live in truth bodily, mentally and spiritually; and as a result creates a very joyous world. When the nations of the world allow love to guide them, they lend financial assistance to other nations of the world that truly needs the funds. In a world where love flows freely, the nations of the world provide world class mental healthcare facilities to other nations of the world to help their citizens that suffer from acute and severe mental health stress and traumas. Also, in a world where love sumptuously abides, the nations of the world also provides for the other nations of the world psych-spiritual trainers that will the people of these other nations when they are attacked spiritually. In a world where love is surplus, when the peoples of the nations of the world come across peoples from the other nations of the world that they relate with in truth, they become very joyful. Their bodies

become stronger as a result of the

meeting and their minds become very

alert. Also, their thoughts become very

active.

Love Isn't Proud And Boastful – Chapter 6

When you love someone, you don't talk about yourself when you're with him. Instead you talk about him. If you love a person, you don't show that you are this or that and that you've this or that. A person who loves another doesn't think less of the person he loves. When you love someone, you don't need to appear important or clever to them. You truly don't need to prove that you are smarter or wiser than them. When you love someone, you don't boast about anything that you've or that you're either bodily, mentally and spiritually. Where love exists between two persons, they always look for ways to shield off any involvement of their material possessions in the relationship between them. When you love someone, money isn't involved in the relationship at all, that is, money isn't a criteria that defines their love. In a relationship where love exists, the persons involved don't show off money to one another but rather, they ensure that the needs of the other person is met. The same is obtainable for mental wise, when love rules the relationship between two persons, they don't show off their level of superiority in understanding to one another, rather they help each other learn the art of self-preservation and logical reasoning. In a situation where two persons love themselves, they don't show off or glory in their height of spirituality. Instead they both help one another reach the level of spirituality that implies eternal life. When a relationship exists between two persons who are boastful, they feel sorrow when they come across each other. Their bodies become weaker and their minds very docile. Their thoughts become active.

The love that exists between a man and a woman makes them do away with any form of competition between them. When a man loves a woman, he doesn't need to appear wise in front of her. The love a man has for a woman makes him talk less about himself and more about the woman when he's with her. When a man loves a woman, he doesn't get to prove to be anything or have anything at all. He doesn't get to display his pride when with her. Where love exists between a man and a woman, they don't boast about anything they possess body wise, mental wise and spiritual wise. If a man loves a woman, he doesn't flaunt his financial status to impress her. When a man loves a woman he doesn't need to use material possessions to show her that he loves her. A man's love for a woman isn't proven by his insatiable quest to show her that he's very intelligent or wise. He doesn't show off any of his mental qualities or milestones. The love that exists between a man and a woman makes the man guide her and heal her spiritually rather than show off how much spiritual powers that he possesses. When a man who shows off a lot is with a woman that he claims to love, he feels sadness. His whole body becomes weaker, his mind become less clear; and his thoughts get very passive.

When love reigns supreme in the family, a father doesn't need to show off himself a more superior being to the mother and children. The father doesn't need to show off his capabilities or acquisitions to the mother and children. Where love takes preeminence the father doesn't feel more important or clever than the mother and children. In a family where love is dominant, the mother doesn't think too highly of herself. The children don't love themselves more than their parents. In a family where love reigns supreme, nobody in the family shows off to the other either bodily, mentally or spiritually. The father never shows off and brags with his material possessions to the mother and children. In a family where love abides, the father doesn't display his superiority of understanding or his mental capabilities to the mother and children. In such a family where love is paramount, no one brags or shows off to another his high spiritual level and mastery. Rather, they all seek to help one another grow and heal spiritually.

In a community where love takes the lead, the members of the community don't want to appear to be smarter or wiser than the other members of the community. Rather, they want to work together with the other members of the community in the unity of love. When love exists in a community, the members of the community don't think too highly of themselves. They also don't love themselves more than they love their community. Instead they love their community as they love themselves. If love rules the affairs of a community, the members of the community don't get to display their abilities or belongings to one another. In a community where love permeates all sphere of existence, the members of the community never talk about their personal achievements to one another. When love guides the affairs of a community, the members of the community don't boast about themselves bodily, mentally and/or spiritually. When love flows freely in the community, the members of the community don't seek to show off their personal financial status or material possessions to the other members of the community as a form of braggadocio. Rather, they seek to help those other members of community who lack the financial resources required to provide themselves with the basic needs of life.

In a community where love precedes everything, the families that make up the community don't show off how much of an understanding those that make up the family possess or how learned they're. When love guides all in a community, the families that make up the community don't show to one another how spiritually advanced they have become. Instead, they help one another become spiritually strong and healthy. As soon as the members of a community where boasting and pride rules the day see one another, they become very sorrowful. Their body become very weak and their thoughts get very active.

Any organization where love is in abundance has members that don't talk about themselves when they are with other members of the organization. They prefer talking about the welfare of other members of the organization than theirs. When love governs an organization, its workers don't try to other workers that they are more capable in their workplace than them. They also don't flaunt their wealth and influence for their fellow workers to see and admire. In an organization where love propels all, the workers in the organization don't attempt to show off their wisdom and cleverness to one another. In such an organization, the workers in no way or form show off either bodily, mentally and spiritually. When love sustains all in an organization, the members of the organization don't show off their assets to other members of the organization. They don't boast in the food, clothes and type of shelter they possess, rather they prefer to give to the others in the organization that suffer hardship. If love guides an organization, the members of the organization don't show off their financial status to other members of the organization. Where love decides in total all that happens in an organization, the workers in the organization don't aim to show to one another how mentally healthy they are than the others. They don't aim to show them that they possess more superior intellect to theirs. In such an organization, the workers don't boast in their psycho-spiritual abilities. Instead, they help those who're afflicted spiritually at the workplace find total guidance, healing and strength. When the members of such an organization where they proudly

boast to one another come across

themselves, they become very unhappy.

Their bodies become weak and their

thoughts very inactive.

A nation where love is valued highly,

has as citizens of the nation, men who

don't aim to show off how smart or wise

or clever they are to the other citizens of

the nation. It has citizens that don't love

themselves more than they love others

and their nation. In such a nation where

love dictates the pace of all things, the citizens of the nation don't brag about their lives and achievements to one another. They don't think too highly of themselves. And as such don't show off to other citizens that they have this or that; and they can do this or that. When love drives the very being of a nation, the citizens of the nation don't need to show off to one another bodily, mentally and/or spiritually. If love is the momentum that accelerates a nation, the government of the nation, don't show off to the citizens of the nation how powerful it can be. The government of such a nation doesn't discard the national constitution and rule by force of authority. Where love exists in a nation, the citizens of the nation don't brag with their monies and material possessions. Rather, they look for ways to help the other citizens of the nation get out of their financial struggles and sufferings. When love directs the rhythm of life in a nation, the citizens of the nation don't show off their academic qualifications or achievements to one another. Instead in love, they help build libraries as well as educational institutions where they can help others reach the pinnacle of their mental powers. In a nation where love abides greatly, the citizens of the nation don't brag about their spiritual level and the strength of the spiritual institutions they have helped built. Instead, they always help the other citizens of the nation find the best spiritual path that shall unite them to deity. When the citizens of such a nation that are proud and boastful meet each other, they feel much angst. Their bodies become weaker and their thoughts become very passive.

If love leads the way in the world, the nations of the world become very wary of the fact that they don't need to show their capabilities to one another. When love takes the front seat in the world, the nations of the world understand that there's no point in always boastfully talking about themselves to other nations of the world. In a world where love is the peak, the nations of the world don't need to prove to one another how sophisticated they are in being clever. If love rules everything in the world, the peoples of the nations of the world always love the peoples of the other nations of the world like they love themselves. They don't think about themselves as being superior to others. When love becomes the leading force of the world, the nations of the world don't show off to one another either bodily, mentally and spiritually. Where love permeates the entire earth, the nations of the world don't show off to the other nations of the world their economic prowess. They don't show off to them the beauty of the infrastructures in their homeland. Rather, they give financial and food relief assistance to the other nations of the world to help them alleviate hunger and poverty. When love becomes the essence of existence in the world, the nations of the world won't show off to other nations of the world how well learned its citizens are or how

mentally superior in understanding its

citizens are. Instead, they help these

other nations of the world become as

learned and educated as they are by

building modern libraries and world

class educational facilities. In such a

world, where love takes preeminence,

the nations of the world always don't

brag to the other nations of the world

about how great and powerful their

spiritual institutions are. Rather, they

gift the other nations of the world with

psycho-spiritual counselors that help man their spiritual centers and provide spiritual healing and guidance to all. In such a world where the nations of the world are proud and boastful, when the peoples of these nations of the world see the peoples of the other nations of the world, they feel much sorrows. Their bodies become very weak and their minds become dulled. Eventually, their thoughts become very passive.

(TO BE CONTINUED….IN PART II)